CREATING GOURD

Sammie Crawford

Photography by **Harry Crawford**

4880 Lower Valley Road • Atglen, PA • 19310

Other Schiffer Books by the Author:
Gourd Fun for Everyone, 978-0-7643-3124-4, $22.99
Holiday Fun: Painting Christmas Gourds, 978-0-7643-3279-1, $14.99

Other Schiffer Books on Related Subjects:
Apples to Apples: Basic Techniques for Decorating Gourds, 978-0-7643-3621-8, $19.99
Gourd Crafts: 6 Projects & Patterns, 978-0-7643-2825-1, $14.95
Decorating Gourds: Carving, Burning, Painting, and More, 0-7643-1312-6, $14.95

Copyright © 2011 by Sammie Crawford
*Unless otherwise noted, all images are the property of the author

Library of Congress Control Number: 2010942309

All rights reserved. No part of this work may be reproduced or used in any form or by any means—graphic, electronic, or mechanical, including photocopying or information storage and retrieval systems—without written permission from the publisher.

The scanning, uploading and distribution of this book or any part thereof via the Internet or via any other means without the permission of the publisher is illegal and punishable by law. Please purchase only authorized editions and do not participate in or encourage the electronic piracy of copyrighted materials.

"Schiffer," "Schiffer Publishing Ltd. & Design," and the "Design of pen and inkwell" are registered trademarks of Schiffer Publishing Ltd.

Designed by Danielle D. Farmer
Cover Design by Bruce Waters
Type set in Zapfino/Arrus BT/Humanist521 BT

ISBN: 978-0-7643-3736-9
Printed in China

PUBLISHING

Schiffer Books are available at special discounts for bulk purchases for sales promotions or premiums. Special editions, including personalized covers, corporate imprints, and excerpts can be created in large quantities forw special needs. For more information contact the publisher:

Published by Schiffer Publishing Ltd.
4880 Lower Valley Road
Atglen, PA 19310

Phone: (610) 593-1777; Fax: (610) 593-2002
E-mail: Info@schifferbooks.com

For the largest selection of fine reference books on this and related subjects, please visit our web site at: www.schifferbooks.com

We are always looking for people to write books on new and related subjects. If you have an idea for a book please contact us at the above address.

This book may be purchased from the publisher.
Include $5.00 for shipping.
Please try your bookstore first.
You may write for a free catalog.

In Europe, Schiffer books are distributed by
Bushwood Books
6 Marksbury Ave.
Kew Gardens
Surrey TW9 4JF England

Phone: 44 (0) 20 8392 8585; Fax: 44 (0) 20 8392 9876
E-mail: info@bushwoodbooks.co.uk
Website: www.bushwoodbooks.co.uk

The gourds came from PumpkinHollow.com and Dalton Farms, 610 CR 336, Piggott, AR 72454; you can contact them through e-mail at ddalton@piggott.net or call 870-598-3568. All paints used in this book are Delta Ceramcoat and the brushes are Loew-Cornell.

ACKNOWLEDGMENTS

Thanks to my editor, Doug Congdon-Martin, and the crew at Schiffer Publishing. It would be hard to find a nicer or more accommodating bunch of folks. They all helped to make this experience a pleasure and worth repeating.

DEDICATION

I dedicate this to the wonderful flying jewels I see in my yard every day. There are rubies (Cardinals), emeralds (Hummingbirds), and sapphires (Bluebirds) — their beauty and melodic songs inspire me. I look forward to their return each spring because they tell me it's time renew and create. I know that the Lord has truly blessed me when I see these wonderful creatures all around me.

CONTENTS

SECTION 1: GETTING STARTED

Preparing the Gourd 8

Painting the Gourd 10

Plywood Bottom Demonstration 16

SECTION 2: THE PROJECTS

Holly Birdhouse 18

Blackberry Birdhouse 24

Lemon Birdhouse... 32

Hacienda Birdhouse... 36

Birch Tree Birdhouse 42

Treehouse Birdhouse....................................... 44

Lily Hat Birdhouse 50

Cat's Head Birdhouse 58

Bumblebee Birdhouse 62

Red Flower Birdfeeder 66

GALLERY 72

GOURD IDENTIFICATION CHART

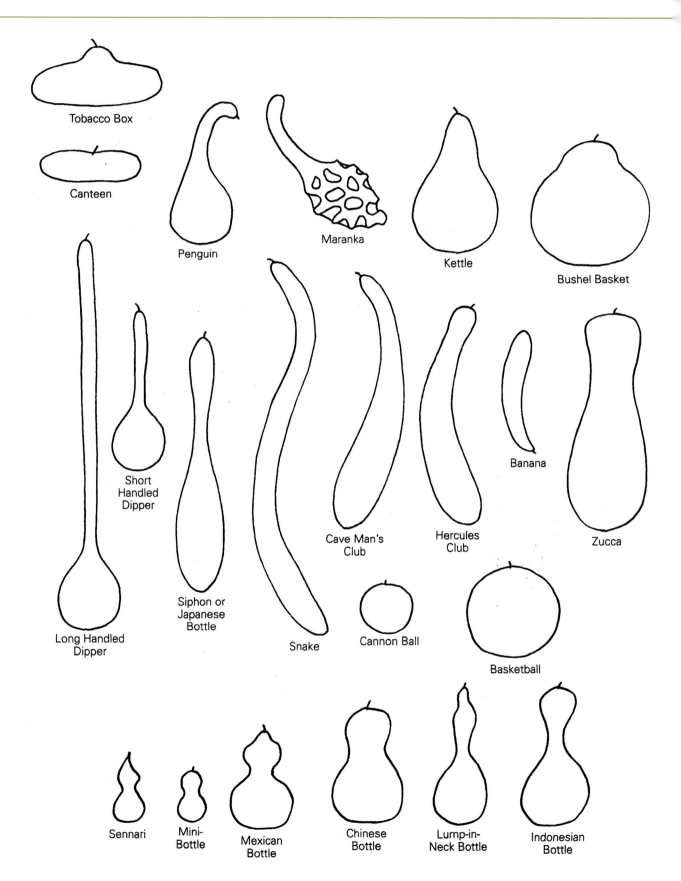

SECTION ONE

Getting Started

PREPARING THE GOURD

Getting Started

Gourds are almost all water when green. To dry out to the stage where we can use them, all that water has to evaporate through the skin. In the process, they turn black and moldy. This is when first time growers throw them away, thinking that they are ruined when actually it's just a necessary step in the process.

When the gourds are light and the seeds rattle (usually), it's time to clean all that mold off. Soak them in the sink in a little water and bleach for a few minutes to soften the mold. They float like corks so turn them occasionally to get them wet all over. Use a plastic scrubber like a Dobie pad and scrub. Remove any stubborn spots with a dull paring knife. Get the gourd completely clean because anything left can flake off later and take all your hard work and paint with it. Once clean and dry, you're ready to begin.

| GETTING STARTED

VARNISHING

Varnishing instructions are the same on each project. When spraying, always allow drying time between coats of varnish. Several light coats are always better than one heavy one because heavy spray can run and ruin your piece. You've spent way too much time making this beautiful piece to get in a hurry now.

SPACKLING AND SANDING

After applying the spackle, dampen your fingers to smooth the edges. Don't use too much water or it will remove the spackle just as too little will. You'll know when you have it right — and don't try to get it perfectly smooth. Sanding will take care of any ridges. Better to apply too much spackle and sand off the excess than to apply too little.

When sanding the spackle, start with medium grit sandpaper like a 150 and then finish with a finer grit like 600. This gives a smooth satin finish and makes your joints undetectable.

As a rule, it's better to sand across the spackle ridges to avoid deepening the valleys between them.

GLUING

A thick layer of wood glue applied to the back of a thin gourd will add strength after drying overnight. The self-leveling glue will also give you a smoother surface to paint. Once the glue dries, you can fill any remaining holes with spackle, then sand, and the inside should be as smooth as the outside.

When adding gourd pieces such as wings to another gourd, try to pick a gourd whose curves match as closely as possible those of the gourd being added to. Not only does this give more surface for gluing, but the pieces are not as likely to be knocked off or broken if they hug the surface of the other gourd.

Your "usual painting supplies" should include tracing paper, transfer paper in black and white, palette paper, a divided water tub or two water containers, Q-tips®, a good grade paper towels, stylus, palette knife, short flexible ruler, kneaded eraser, sponge, pencil and charcoal and chalk pencils. In addition, I usually keep a bottle of blending gel in my tote. Keeping these things stocked in a divided plastic tote makes it easier to pack for classes, etc. You only have to add the brushes and paints you'll need and you're ready to go.

Terminology

Don't be confused by the terms used here. These are some of the most common terms and their definitions:

Float, shade, and sideload:

These all mean the same thing. This is when you load paint onto the corner of your brush and blend it to paint a shadow or highlight.

Retarder, extender, and blending gel:

Three more words that are the same — this is just a medium used to give you a longer open time, to extend the drying time so you can work the paint longer.

Wash:

This is 90% water and 10% paint and is used to soften when your shade or highlight may be too stark. The wash helps unite the base, shadows, and highlights.

1 | GETTING STARTED

Painting Stroke Illustrations
Floating or Side-loading a Brush

Use at least a #12 or 1/2" wide brush. Moisten the brush with clean water and blot on a paper towel just until it loses its sheen. Leave as much water without it being drippy.

Holding it at a 45-degree angle, dip the corner of the brush in the paint.

Apply a slight pressure and work the brush back and forth on the palette. Be careful not to let the paint get on the clean side of the brush.

Flip the brush over and gently pinch off the water from the brush. Some people don't do this, but I find I have a "halo" along the edge of my float if I don't.

PAINTING THE GOURD

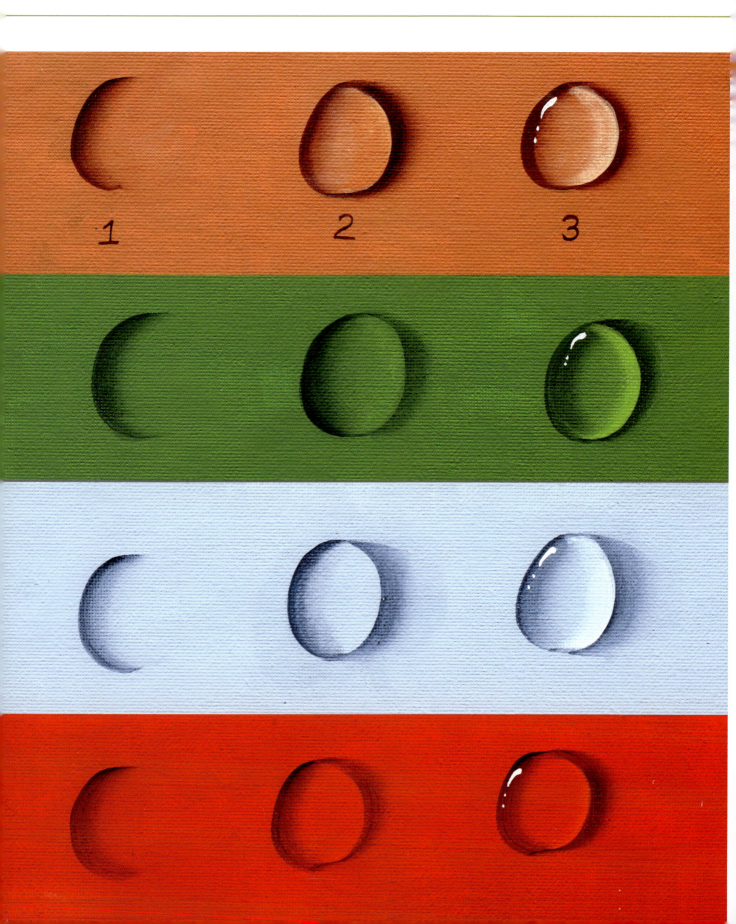

1 | GETTING STARTED

OTHER WAYS TO FLOAT

There is more than one way to float. If you are having difficulty getting a nice, smooth float, try one of these methods.

1. Moisten the surface with water before floating. Don't flood it, just dampen it.

2. If that doesn't do it, try blending gel. Use a separate brush to paint the area with blending gel before floating then float as usual.

3. If these two methods don't yield the desired result, try double loading your brush. Dress the entire brush in your base color then dip the corner in the color you're floating with. Work the brush back and forth to blend the two colors just as you would for a regular float and paint.

WATER DROPS

1. Use the #12 flat and your shading color to float a "C" stroke counterclockwise from 12:00 to 6:00.

2. Without turning the brush, use the same color to float a reverse C stroke clockwise from 12:00 to 6:00 to complete the circle.

3. On the inside of the circle, use your highlight color to float a C stroke back to back to your second float. Use the liner brush to add a white comma inside on the dark side.

Painting Stroke Illustrations

Using a Liner Brush

When using a liner brush, always thin the paint to the consistency of milk or ink. Do this by pulling a small amount of paint over to a drop of water on your palette. (If you don't thin it, the paint will not flow off the brush tip.)

When the brush is dressed, pull the point back in shape by rotating the brush between your fingers as you pull it across the palette. Regular liners are fine for comma strokes, but if you are making long lines, try using a script liner.

Using Your Rake Brush

Moisten your brush and blot on a paper towel just until it loses its shine. Dress the brush with paint and work it back and forth on the palette. Set the brush down on the palette and fan the bristles by applying slight pressure and rotating the brush between your fingers. But don't let the metal ferrule touch because it can cut the bristles off.

If you have the correct amount of water and paint in your brush, light strokes will produce fine lines. Too much or too little water and it makes a solid stroke. It's just a matter of practice. Once you find the balance, you will really enjoy making hair, beards, and fur.

| GETTING STARTED

OTHER USEFUL TIPS

- Close your eyes and run your fingers over the piece when you are doing that final sanding. You will feel things your eyes missed and you'll get a much smoother finish.

- Keep a dampened cotton swab handy for an eraser. Go ahead and dampen and squeeze dry both ends because when you need it, you don't have time to figure out which end is wet.

- When sponging, turn your sponge frequently to avoid a "cookie cutter" look unless you are going for a specific pattern.

- Always use your mop brush dry. To remove excess paint during a process, rub the brush in a circular motion on a damp spot of your paper towel. Only wash it completely when you are finished with it.

Plywood Bottom Demonstration

Here are some basic instructions for making a plywood bottom.

Place the gourd on the plywood and draw around it. Mark the gourd and the board so they can be matched up once the cut is made.

Allowing for the thickness of the gourd, draw a second line inside the first one. This will be your cutting line.

Make the cut. Notice the mark has been extended into the circle so it won't be lost when the circle is cut.

Mark the inside with an "X" and then extend the mark on the side to the other side of the wood.

Align the marks and try the piece for fit. It probably won't fit on the first try, so sand where needed until it does. Add any needed weight at this point. I use buckshot or kitty litter to add stability.

Spackle any cracks and sand smooth when dry. Paint as you would the rest of the gourd.

SECTION TWO

The Projects

HOLLY BIRDHOUSE

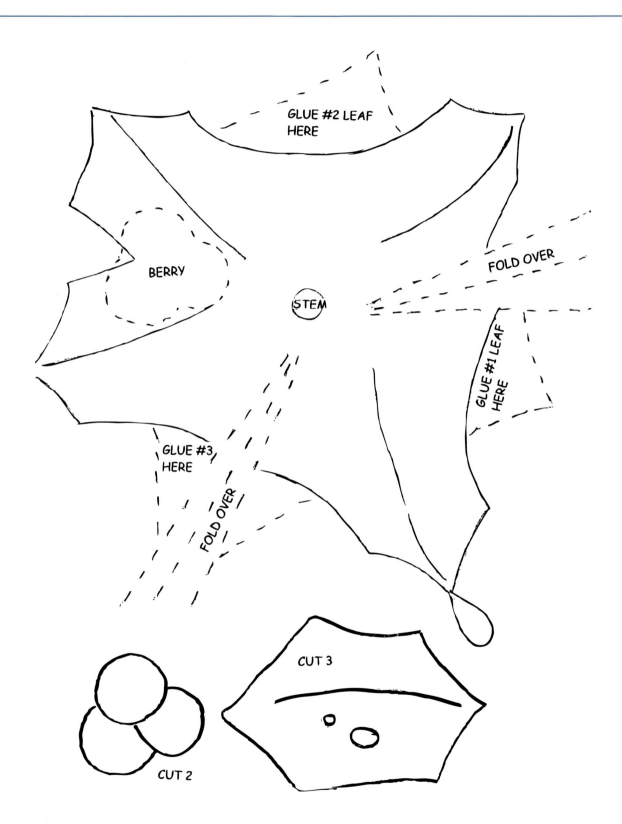

Because of the unique nature of gourds, these patterns may have to be altered to fit each individual gourd. You may enlarge, shrink or alter them in any way necessary to make them work for you. To view over one hundred gourd patterns, visit her website TheFairyGourdmother.com.

| THE PROJECTS

Holly Birdhouse

PALETTE

Black Cherry ~ Tangerine ~ Burnt Sienna ~ Opaque Red ~ White ~ Black ~ Dark Foliage ~ Medium Foliage ~ Light Foliage ~ Liberty Blue

BRUSHES

Series 7300 #12 flat ~ Series 7350 10/0 liner ~ Series 7550 1" wash brush ~ #275 1/2" mop

SUPPLIES

8" cannonball gourd ~ Craft saw ~ 1/4" drill bit and drill ~ 1 1/2" hole saw ~ Scrap gourd pieces ~ 1/4" dowel, 3" long ~ Wood glue ~ Gloss spray varnish

Assembly

Trace the pattern and cut three leaves and two sets of berries from the scrap gourds. Try to match the pieces to the curve of the gourd you will be gluing them to. They look better when they follow the shape of the gourd and are more securely fastened. Use the hole saw to cut the entry hole. Use the 1/4" drill bit for the perch hole.

Painting the Piece

Using the wash brush, basecoat the loose leaves and the ones on top of the gourd with Dark Foliage. Apply pattern to gourd top.

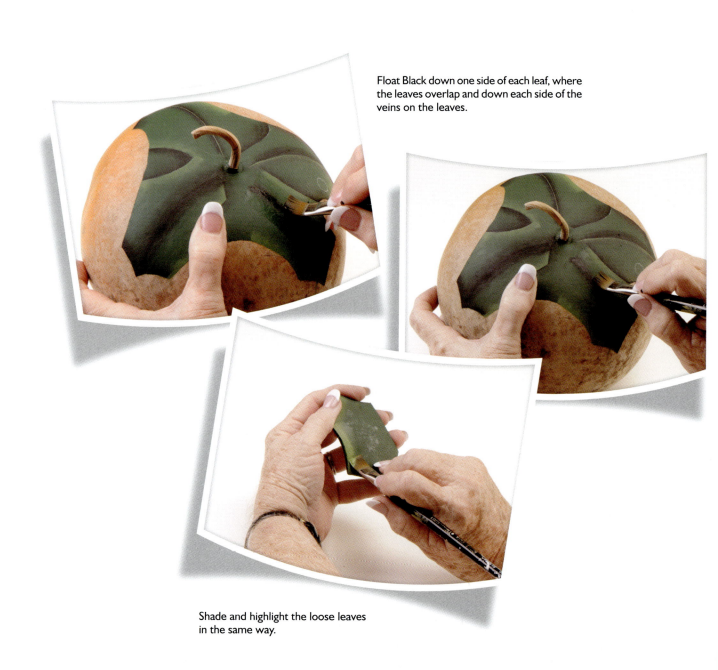

Float Black down one side of each leaf, where the leaves overlap and down each side of the veins on the leaves.

Shade and highlight the loose leaves in the same way.

| THE PROJECTS

Shade and highlight the loose leaves in the same way.

Use the liner brush and Light Foliage to highlight the veins.

Basecoat the berries with Opaque Red. Float a shade of Black Cherry on one side and where they overlap.

Float a Tangerine highlight on the opposite sides.

Float a little Liberty Blue over the Black as a reflected light.

HOLLY BIRDHOUSE

Barely moisten the surface and tap a little White onto the center of each berry.

Quickly mop to soften the white to a blurred highlight.

Reference the text in the Introduction on water drops for details. Float a "C" stroke counterclockwise from 12 to 6 o'clock. Place the brush back at 12 and complete the circle with a reverse "C" stroke clockwise to 6 o'clock. Keep the brush in the flat position, never turning the brush as you stroke.

Turn the leaf upside down and, on the clean side inside the drop, float a counterclockwise White "C" stroke.

On the side opposite the White "C" stroke, use the liner brush to place a White comma stroke.

2 | THE PROJECTS

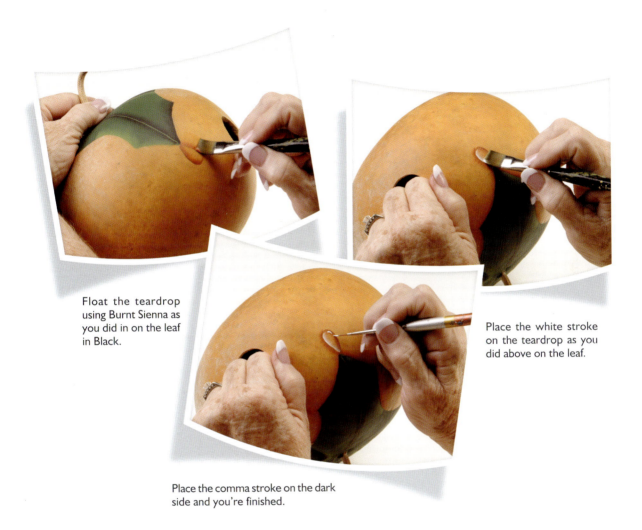

Float the teardrop using Burnt Sienna as you did in on the leaf in Black.

Place the white stroke on the teardrop as you did above on the leaf.

Place the comma stroke on the dark side and you're finished.

To finish, float Burnt Sienna around all the leaves painted on top of the gourd. Glue the leaves and berries in place and finish with several light coats of varnish.

BLACKBERRY BIRDHOUSE

Trace ONLY the part of the pattern with the solid lines. Paint these leaves and berries on top of the gourd. Use the dotted lines as a guide to attach the add-on pieces.

Because of the unique nature of gourds, these patterns may have to be altered to fit each individual gourd. You may enlarge, shrink or alter them in any way necessary to make them work for you. To view over one hundred gourd patterns, visit her website TheFairyGourdmother.com.

2 | THE PROJECTS

Blackberry Birdhouse

PALETTE

Autumn Brown ~ Butter Yellow ~ Light Foliage ~ Medium Foliage ~ Dark Foliage ~ Dusty Mauve ~ Sachet ~ Black ~ White ~ Raspberry ~ Colonial Blue ~ Black Cherry

BRUSHES

Series 7300 #12 flat ~ Series 7350 10/0 liner ~ Series 7500 #6 filbert

SUPPLIES

7-8" diameter round gourd ~ Gourd scraps ~ 1/4" dowel, 3" long ~ 1 1/2" hole saw ~ 1/4" drill bit and drill ~ Wood glue ~ Gloss spray varnish

Assembling the Piece

Use the hole saw to drill the entry hole and clean the gourd out. Use the 1/4" drill bit to drill the hole for the perch. Trace the patterns on the gourd scraps and cut three leaves, two single berries, and one triple berry.

BLACKBERRY BIRDHOUSE

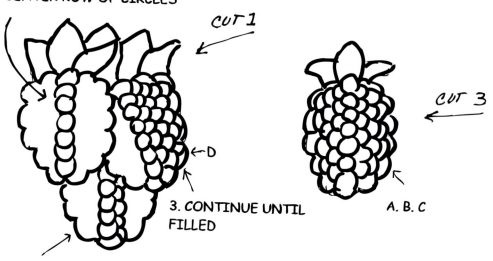

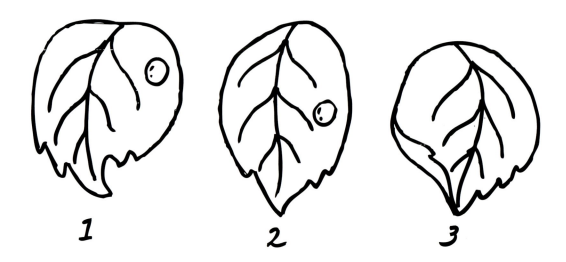

CUT ONE OF EACH LEAF

Because of the unique nature of gourds, these patterns may have to be altered to fit each individual gourd. You may enlarge, shrink or alter them in any way necessary to make them work for you. To view over one hundred gourd patterns, visit her website TheFairyGourdmother.com.

2 | THE PROJECTS

Painting the Piece

Apply the pattern to the top of the gourd and basecoat all the leaves Medium Foliage. Basecoat the lighter berries with Raspberry and the darker ones with Black Cherry.

Use the #12 flat and Dark Foliage to shade down one edge of the leaves, anywhere they flip over and down each side of the veins in the leaves.

Float Light Foliage down the opposite side of the leaves.

Further enhance the highlight by using Butter Yellow along the edges, leaving some of the first color showing.

BLACKBERRY BIRDHOUSE

Use the liner brush and Light Foliage to highlight the veins

Use the liner and Black Cherry to draw circles on the light berries.

Use the #12 flat and Black Cherry to shade the bottom of each circle.

Mix Raspberry and White 1:1 and highlight the top two-thirds of the left half of the berries.

Highlight the top one-third of that same side with Sachet.

2 | THE PROJECTS

Use the liner brush and White to place highlight dots on some of the lightest places.

Float Colonial Blue on the bottom one-third of the right side of the berries as a reflected light.

Mix Black Cherry and Black 4:1 and use the liner brush to draw circles on the dark berries. Use the #12 flat and the same mix to shade the bottoms of each circle. On the top two-thirds of the left side of each berry, highlight with Dusty Mauve across the tops of the circles.

On the top one-third of the same side, highlight the tops of the circles with Sachet.

Use the liner brush and White to place a dot on several of the lighter floats near the top of the berry.

Float Colonial Blue on the lower one-third of the right side of the berries as reflected light. Don't overdo this step.

BLACKBERRY BIRDHOUSE

Float Dark Foliage across the bottoms and between the calyxes.

Highlight the tops of the calyxes with Light Foliage.

Use the liner brush and Dark Foliage for the veins.

2 | THE PROJECTS

For directions on the water drops, see water drops in Getting Started.

To finish, glue the leaves, berries, and perch in place. Spray with several light coats of varnish.

LEMON BIRDHOUSE

Because of the unique nature of gourds, these patterns may have to be altered to fit each individual gourd. You may enlarge, shrink or alter them in any way necessary to make them work for you. To view over one hundred gourd patterns, visit her website TheFairyGourdmother.com.

| THE PROJECTS

Lemon Birdhouse

PALETTE

White ~ Luscious Lemon ~ Opaque Yellow ~ Light Foliage

BRUSHES

Series 7300 #6, #12 flats ~ Series 7350 10/0 liner ~ Series 7550 1" wash brush

SUPPLIES

Strawberry gourd ~ 1/4" plywood scrap ~ 1 1/2" hole saw ~ 1/4" drill bit and drill ~ Craft saw ~ Sea sponge ~ Wood glue ~ 1/4" dowel, 3" long ~ Short piece of rawhide thong ~ Gloss spray varnish

Assembling the Piece

Cut the gourd in half and clean out. Use the 1/4" drill to make a hole in the edge of the gourd for the hanger. Lay the gourd on the plywood and draw around it. Cut out the plywood circle and use the hole saw to make the entry hole. Drill a 1/4" hole for the perch just under the entry hole. Glue the plywood to the gourd and allow to dry several hours or overnight.

LEMON BIRDHOUSE

Painting the Piece

Use the wash brush to basecoat the entire piece White. When dry, paint with Luscious Lemon. When dry, sponge Opaque Yellow over the gourd part.

Apply the pattern and use the #6 and White to paint the membranes.

Use the liner brush to paint the seed White.

| THE PROJECTS

Use the #12 and Light Foliage to shade down one side of the seeds and against the membranes in some of the yellow sections.

Now, paint the perch White and glue in place. Knot one end of the thong, then thread it up through the hole in the gourd. Tie a loop to create a hanger. Finish with several light coats of varnish.

HACIENDA BIRDHOUSE

Because of the unique nature of gourds, these patterns may have to be altered to fit each individual gourd. You may enlarge, shrink or alter them in any way necessary to make them work for you. To view over one hundred gourd patterns, visit her website TheFairyGourdmother.com.

| THE PROJECTS

Hacienda Birdhouse

PALETTE

Ivory ~ Georgia Clay ~ Pigskin ~ Trail ~ Red Iron Oxide ~ Black ~ Azure Blue ~ Burnt Sienna ~ Black Green ~ Alpine Green ~ White ~ Rooster Red

BRUSHES

Series 7300 #8, #12 brushes ~ Series 7350 10/0 liner ~ Series 7500 #6 filbert ~ Series 7550 1" wash brush

SUPPLIES

7-9" martinhouse gourd ~ Sea sponge ~ Chalk pencil ~ 1 1/2" hole saw ~ Drill ~ 1/4" dowel, 3" long (optional) ~ 1/4" drill bit (optional) ~ Satin spray varnish

Assembling the Piece

Use the hole saw to drill the entry hole and clean the gourd out. *Optional: Use the 1/4" drill bit to make the hole for the perch under the first hole.*

Painting the Piece

Draw a chalk line around the gourd for the roof line. Use the 1" wash brush to basecoat the house Ivory and the roof Georgia Clay. Sponge Trail over the Ivory to give a stucco effect.

Use the #12 flat and Red Iron Oxide for the roof tiles, starting in the back just in case you come out uneven.

Use the #8 and Georgia Clay to randomly place bricks around the sides of the house. Use care to keep them level.

2 | THE PROJECTS

Use the liner brush and Black to outline the bottom and one side of the bricks. These don't need to be perfect. Use a painterly stroke.

Repeat the outlines on the bottom and one side of the shingles.

Paint the door and fence with Pigskin, using the #12 for the door and a smaller brush for the fence.

Use the #12 and Burnt Sienna to shade the boards on the door.

HACIENDA BIRDHOUSE

The hinges, nails, and door handle are done in Black using the liner brush.

Use the filbert and Alpine to paint the cactus.

Shade the cactus with Black Green where the sections meet or cross over.

2 | THE PROJECTS

Use the liner brush to place little Black Green "v's" all over the cactus.

The chili peppers are made using the liner brush and Rooster Red.

Birch Tree Birdhouse

PALETTE

Raw Linen ~ Burnt Sienna ~ Dark Burnt Umber

BRUSHES

Series 7300 #12 flat ~ Series 7350 10/0 liner ~ Series 7550 1" wash brush

SUPPLIES

Large, cylindrical gourd ~ Any gourd with a pointed top ~ 1/4" plywood scrap ~ Wood glue ~ 1 1/2" hole saw ~ Drill ~ DAP Fast n' Final spackle ~ Medium grit sandpaper ~ Dark chalk pencil

Assembling the Piece

Cut a section of the long gourd any length you want to but a minimum of six inches tall. Cut the top off the other gourd at a point where it is wide enough to make the roof of the birdhouse. Glue the top on.

Use the hole saw to cut the entry hole. Place the house on the plywood and draw around it. See the demonstration in the Introduction for fitting the plywood bottom in place. Spackle any cracks once the bottom is in place and sand smooth when dry.

2 | THE PROJECTS

Painting the Piece

Use the wash brush to paint the entire piece Raw Linen. On the roof, draw lines from top to bottom to indicate slices of tree. Use the #12 flat to make back to back Dark Burnt Umber floats, following the chalk lines.

Use the liner brush and the same color to make horizontal lines on the roof and sides and the heart on the tree. Use care to keep your lines straight and level. By varying the pressure on the brush as you pull it along, you will get the thick and thin lines.

Use the #12 flat and Burnt Sienna to float around the hole.

Float Dark Burnt Umber around the hole, leaving some of the Burnt Sienna showing.

Use the chisel edge of your brush to pull radiating lines outward from the hole to make it look more like a knot hole.

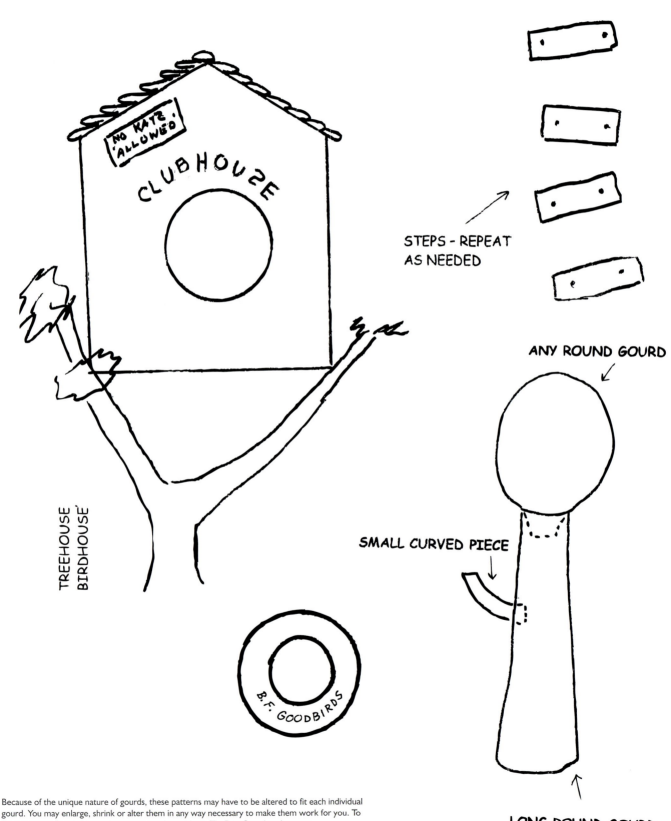

Because of the unique nature of gourds, these patterns may have to be altered to fit each individual gourd. You may enlarge, shrink or alter them in any way necessary to make them work for you. To view over one hundred gourd patterns, visit her website TheFairyGourdmother.com.

2 | THE PROJECTS

Treehouse Birdhouse

PALETTE

Spice Tan ~ Spice Brown ~ Flesh Tan ~ Latte ~ Light Foliage ~ Medium Foliage ~ Dark Foliage ~ Black ~ White

BRUSHES

Series 7300 #8, #12 flats ~ Series 7350 10/0 liner ~ Series 7550 1" wash brush

SUPPLIES

Long, cylindrical gourd ~ Small curved gourd piece ~ Dipper gourd or any round gourd ~ Sponge ~ String ~ Wood glue ~ DAP Fast n' Final spackle ~ Medium grit sandpaper ~ 1/4" plywood scrap ~ Craft saw ~ Spray varnish

Assembling the Piece

To fit the bottom of the piece with a plywood bottom, see the demonstration in the introduction. Cut the handle off the dipper gourd and glue the ball section to the top of the long gourd. Cut a small hole in the side of the long gourd and glue the small curved piece in place to make a limb. Spackle all joints and, when dry, sand smooth.

To make a swing, cut a small circle about the size of a lifesaver candy and drill a hole in the center. Sand the outer edges round so it resembles a tire.

TREEHOUSE BIRDHOUSE

Painting the Piece

Basecoat the tree trunk Spice Tan and then sponge Dark Foliage on the top portion. Keep the color ragged where the two colors meet.

When dry, sponge Medium Foliage, leaving some of the darker green showing. Repeat with Light Foliage only on the top one-third of the greenery. Pull some limbs up into the foliage.

Paint the clubhouse Latte.

Use the chisel edge of the #12 flat and Spice Brown to paint the bark on the trunk.

Use the same brush and color to float the boards on the clubhouse and under the roofline.

Use the liner and Spice Brown to make the woodgrain on the boards.

Use the #8 flat and Spice Tan to make the ladder on the trunk.

TREEHOUSE BIRDHOUSE

Pull a shadow along the bottom and up one side of each step using the liner brush and Spice Brown.

Use the same color and the stylus to make the nails on the steps.

Highlight the steps across the top and down the opposite side from the shadow using Flesh Tan and the #12 flat.

| THE PROJECTS

Use the #12 flat and White to paint the sign.

The lettering on the clubhouse and sign are done with the liner brush and Black.

The lettering on the clubhouse and sign are done with the liner brush and Black.

Sponge a little Medium Foliage over the edges of the clubhouse. Paint the tire Black. The lettering, "B.F. Goodbirds" is White. Tie it to the limb with the string. Finish with several light coats of varnish.

LILY HAT BIRDHOUSE

Because of the unique nature of gourds, these patterns may have to be altered to fit each individual gourd. You may enlarge, shrink or alter them in any way necessary to make them work for you. To view over one hundred gourd patterns, visit her website TheFairyGourdmother.com.

2 | THE PROJECTS

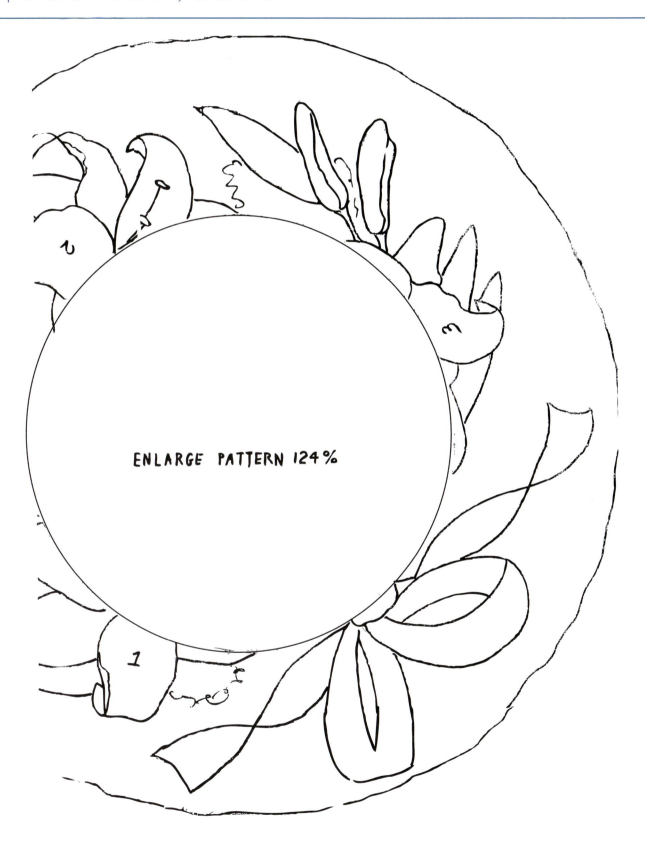

LILY HAT BIRDHOUSE

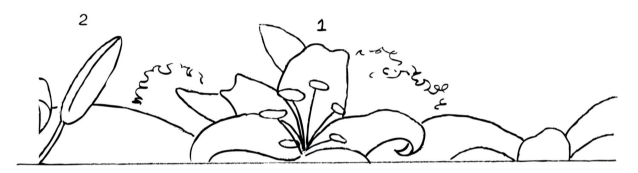

ENLARGE PATTERNS 124%

Because of the unique nature of gourds, these patterns may have to be altered to fit each individual gourd. You may enlarge, shrink or alter them in any way necessary to make them work for you. To view over one hundred gourd patterns, visit her website TheFairyGourdmother.com.

2 | THE PROJECTS

Lily Hat Birdhouse

Palette

Lichen Grey ~ Toffee ~ White ~ Opaque Yellow ~ Butter ~ Red Iron Oxide ~ Dark Foliage ~ Medium Foliage ~ Light Foliage ~ Straw ~ Coral

Brushes

Series 7300 #2, 12 flats ~ Series 7350 10/0 liner ~ Series 7500 #8 filbert ~ Series 7520 1/2" filbert rake ~ Series 7550 1" wash brush ~ #275 1/2" mop

Supplies

7" round gourd ~ 8" square of 1/4" scrap plywood ~ 13" circle of 1/4" plywood ~ 1 1/2" hole saw ~ 1/4" wooden dowel, 3" long ~ 1/4" drill bit and drill ~ Wood glue ~ Craft saw ~ Fine grit sandpaper ~ Stylus ~ White chalk pencil ~ Sea sponge ~ Blending gel

Assembling the Piece

Cut the gourd in half and clean the inside. Center the gourd on the 13" circle and glue in place. Use the hole saw to cut the entry hole then use the 1/4" drill bit to drill a hole for the perch. Don't glue the perch in until you've painted the piece.

Painting the Piece

Use the wash brush to basecoat the entire piece with Lichen. Apply the pattern by matching the numbers on the flowers. If the pattern doesn't quite fit, evenly space the three lilies around the hat and fill in with leaves and sponged greenery as needed. Basecoat the lilies White and then over paint with a mix of Straw and White 2:1. Basecoat the ribbon Red Iron Oxide and the leaves and stems Medium Foliage. Use the chalk pencil to draw the circles about 1" apart around the hat.

Use the #12 flat and Toffee to float shaky shadows fading away from the crown following the chalk lines. Also shade under the flowers and leaves.

Use the rake brush and the same color to stroke lines between the circles.

2 | THE PROJECTS

Use the liner brush and Brown Iron Oxide to make squiggly broken lines along the shading.

Use the #12 flat to shade the ribbon with a mix of Red Iron Oxide and Black 6:1.

Apply the blending gel and highlight the ribbon with back to back floats of Coral.

Mop to soften the floats.

Highlight the upper edges of the ribbons with Coral.

Use the #12 flat and Dark Foliage to shade the leaves on the bottom edges, on top of the veins and where they go under other leaves and objects.

LILY HAT BIRDHOUSE

Highlight the leaves with Light Foliage along the top edges, below the veins and opposite the shading where they go under other leaves.

Use the #12 flat and Antique Gold to shade the lilies and buds.

Use the #12 flat and Antique Gold to shade down each side of the veins.

Highlight the lilies with White.

Deepen some of the shadows on the lilies using Red Iron Oxide.

Mop to soften and blend.

Use the liner brush and Light Foliage to paint the stamen stems.

Use the liner brush to make Brown Iron Oxide "sit down" strokes on the ends.

Float a little Light Foliage at the base of the buds.

Deepen some of the shadows on the buds using Red Iron Oxide.

Use the liner and White to highlight the veins.

Glue the perch in place and finish with several light coats of varnish.

CAT'S HEAD BIRDHOUSE

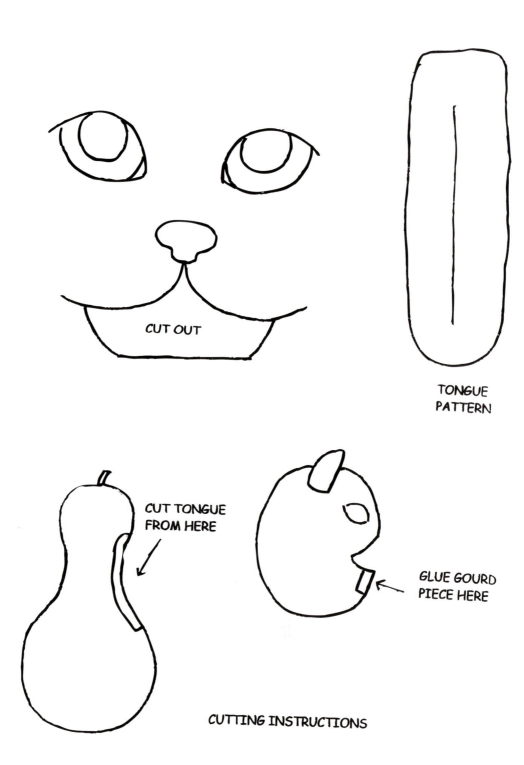

Because of the unique nature of gourds, these patterns may have to be altered to fit each individual gourd. You may enlarge, shrink or alter them in any way necessary to make them work for you. To view over one hundred gourd patterns, visit her website TheFairyGourdmother.com.

2 | THE PROJECTS

Cat's Head Birdhouse

PALETTE

Quaker Grey ~ Hippo Grey ~ Charcoal ~ Butter ~ Custard ~ Black ~ White ~ Rouge ~ Red Iron Oxide ~ Candy Bar Brown ~ Bouquet

BRUSHES

Series 7000 #6 round ~ Series 7300 #12 flat ~ Series 7350 10/0 liner ~ Series 7520 1/2" filbert rake ~ Series 7550 1" wash

SUPPLIES

5-6" dia. cannonball gourd ~ Dipper gourd handle ~ Gourd pieces ~ X-acto knife ~ Craft store whiskers ~ Coat hanger or craft wire ~ Pliers ~ Wire cutters ~ Craft saw ~ Wood glue ~ 1/8" drill bit and drill ~ Clamp

Assembling the Piece

Apply the pattern and use the craft saw to cut the mouth opening. Measure the width of the tongue and be sure the bottom of the mouth is flat where the tongue will be glued.

Cut the end of the dipper gourd handle in half for the ears. Trace the tongue pattern and cut from scrap gourd. Drill a hole in the top of the head for the hanger. Clean the gourd out and glue the ears in place.

Cut a small piece of gourd and glue inside the mouth at the bottom. Clamp until dry. This will give more surface for the tongue to stick to.

Painting the Piece

Use the wash brush to basecoat the entire gourd Quaker Grey.

Use the rake brush and Hippo Grey to make the fur. Add random strokes of Charcoal for accent. Stroke a little White on the muzzle as well.

Paint the eyes Butter Yellow with Black pupils.

Paint the nose Hippo Grey and use the #12 flat and Charcoal to float around the edges, fading toward the center of the nose.

Use the wash brush to basecoat the tongue Rouge.

Paint the back of the tongue Candy Bar Brown, fading into the Rouge. This helps set the tongue back in the head and hides the end.

Use the #12 and Red iron Oxide to place a back to back float down the center of the tongue.

Paint the inside of the ears with Bouquet.

Float around the mouth and under the eyes with Charcoal.

Use the liner brush and Custard to pull radiating lines from the pupils. Use caution to keep the lines straight. It helps to place lines at 3, 6, and 9 o'clock and then fill in between.

Place a Black float across the tops of the eyes and extending slightly beyond the outer edges.

Use the liner brush to place White comma strokes in the eyes and on the top of the nose.

To finish, cut a length of wire and bend one end into a tight curl. Thread it up through the mouth and out the top of the gourd. Bend this end into a curl for hanging. Glue the tongue in place and spray with several light coats of varnish.

BUMBLEBEE BIRDHOUSE

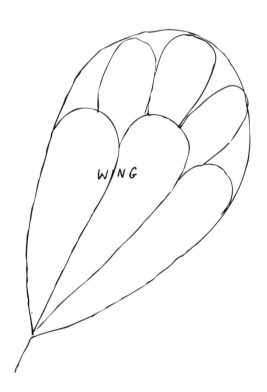

Because of the unique nature of gourds, these patterns may have to be altered to fit each individual gourd. You may enlarge, shrink or alter them in any way necessary to make them work for you. To view over one hundred gourd patterns, visit her website TheFairyGourdmother.com.

Bumblebee Birdhouse

PALETTE

Yellow ~ Leaf Green ~ White ~ Black

BRUSHES

Series 7300 #12 flat ~ Series 7350 10/0 liner ~ Series 7550 1" wash brush ~ Series 7850 1/2" deerfoot

SUPPLIES

Medium bottle gourd ~ Yellow cellophane ~ Glue gun ~ 4 black chenilles ~ 1 bumpy black chenille ~ 1/4" dowel, 3" long ~ 1/4" drill bit and drill ~ 1 1/2" hole saw ~ Craft glue ~ Chalk pencil ~ Black permanent marker ~ Scissors ~ Satin spray varnish

Assembling the Piece

Use the hole saw to drill the entry hole. Use the 1/4" drill bit to drill holes for the wings, feelers, and perch.

BUMBLEBEE BIRDHOUSE

Painting the Piece

Use the 1" wash brush to undercoat the body White. When dry, paint it Yellow and the head Black. Use the chalk pencil to draw horizontal lines around the body.

Use the deerfoot (or an old scruffy brush) to paint the stripes Black.

Apply the face pattern and use the liner brush and White to outline the features.

Use the #12 and White to float the eyelids and the nose.

Float Leaf Green in the eyes.

THE PROJECTS

Use the liner brush and White for the comma strokes in the eyes and the lashes. Finish with several light coats of varnish.

Use the pattern to bend the four chenilles to the right shape. Apply hot glue to one wing.

Quickly place the cellophane over the wing.

Apply glue over the cellophane and place the second wing on top of the first one.

Cut away the excess cellophane.

Place the wing over the pattern and draw in the sections with the marker. Cut two "bumps" from the bumpy chenille. Glue them on for antennas and glue the wings and perch in place.

RED FLOWER BIRDFEEDER

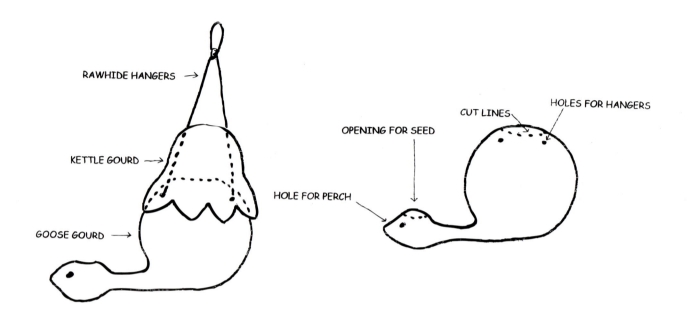

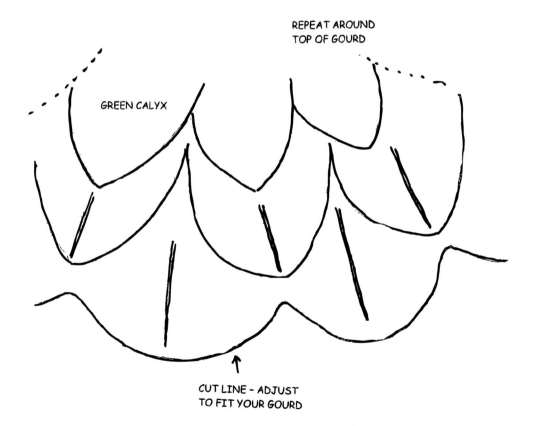

Because of the unique nature of gourds, these patterns may have to be altered to fit each individual gourd. You may enlarge, shrink or alter them in any way necessary to make them work for you. To view over one hundred gourd patterns, visit her website TheFairyGourdmother.com.

2 | THE PROJECTS

Red Flower Birdfeeder

PALETTE

Black Cherry ~ Roman Stucco ~ Dark Foliage ~ Light Foliage ~ Medium Foliage ~ Opaque Red ~ Tangerine ~ White

BRUSHES

Series 7300 #12 flat ~ Series 7350 10/0 liner ~ Series 7550 1" wash

SUPPLIES

Goose gourd ~ Kettle gourd ~ 2 26" long rawhide thongs ~ 1 12" long rawhide thong ~ Craft saw ~ Coat hanger ~ 1/4" dowel, 6" long ~ 1/4" drill bit and drill ~ 1/4" brass eyelets ~ Wood glue ~ Gloss spray varnish

Assembling the Piece

Cut the kettle gourd at the widest point and apply the flower pattern. Cut the scalloped edge. Cut a hole in the side of the goose gourd large enough to clean the gourd out. See the diagram. Cut another hole about the size of a quarter in the bulb of the gourd. Drill a couple of drain holes on the opposite side of the bulb. Drill a hole through the bulb per diagram for the perch. Use the coat hanger bent double to clean the neck of the gourd out so seeds can pass through. Drill four evenly spaced holes in the flower gourd. Set the flower in place on the other gourd and mark the four holes on the bottom gourd. Drill a matching set of holes in the bottom gourd. Mark one hole so it can be matched up later.

RED FLOWER BIRDFEEDER

Painting the Piece

Use the wash brush to basecoat the flower Opaque Red and the upper part Medium Foliage. Use the #12 flat and Dark Foliage to shade where the pieces overlap and to pull lines near the stem end.

Use Light Foliage to highlight opposite the darker floats.

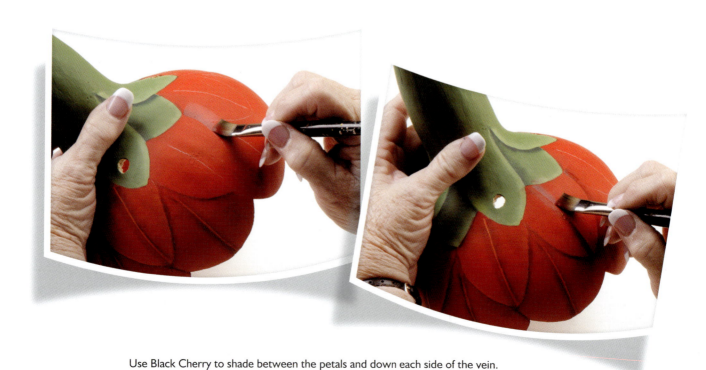

Use Black Cherry to shade between the petals and down each side of the vein.

2 | THE PROJECTS

Float Tangerine on the petals for highlight.

Use Tangerine and the liner brush to highlight the veins.

RED FLOWER BIRDFEEDER

Use the wash brush to basecoat the lower gourd Roman Stucco.

Paint the perch Light Foliage and glue in place. Finish with several light coats of varnish.

Place the brass eyelets in the eight holes, gluing if necessary.

2 | THE PROJECTS

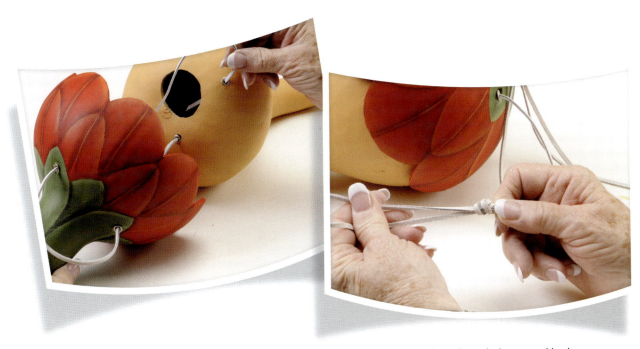

Tie a knot in the end of a long thong and thread it through the tan gourd, up through the top and back down into the bottom gourd again. Tie a knot in that end and repeat these steps with the second thong.

Tie the shorter thong into a loop and then loop the shorter thong through the other two loops to create a hanger.

GALLERY

GALLERY

GALLERY

GALLERY

"The Four Seasons"

Patterns for Spring and Fall are available at the **FairyGourdmother.com**

GALLERY

GALLERY

GALLERY

GALLERY

GALLERY